Know Your RIGHTS!

LA's Sex Crime Defense Guide

Ronald D. Hedding, Esq.

Speakeasy Publishing
73-03 Bell Blvd, #10
Oakland Gardens, NY 11364
www.speakeasypublishinginc.com

Ordering Information:

Quantity sales. Special discounts are available on quantity purchases by corporations, associations, and others. For details, contact the publisher at the address above.

Orders by U.S. trade bookstores and wholesalers. Please contact Speakeasy Publishing: Tel: (888) 991-2766 or visit www.speakeasypublishinginc.com.

Printed in the United States of America.

Published in 2017.

ISBN: 978-1-946481-43-6

FOREWORD

This book is meant to assist the reader in understanding some of the issues that come up in sex crime cases. It addresses some of the most common questions that I have seen come up over the course of the last 25 years that I have been defending individuals who've been charged with sex-related offenses. This book does not cover every possible issue that can arise in a sex crime case, but it is certainly a foundation to begin to understand and deal with those important issues that will come up in a sex crime case.

I have represented clients for just about every sex-related offense in the California Penal Code and have successfully litigated many jury trials all over California, including Los Angeles, Orange County, Ventura, San Bernardino and Riverside. If the book does not answer all of your questions and you or a loved one has a sex crime case pending, call me directly and we can meet to discuss the case. I can provide you with the answers you seek and a plan for moving forward to resolve your matter.

DEDICATION

This book is dedicated to those individuals who find that they are facing a sometimes unforgiving criminal justice system, who are scared and looking for answers. It has been my experience that once you begin to educate yourself on how the system works and what you are up against, you begin to take back control of your fate and start the process of getting out of the system and moving on with your life.

It is my experience that with certainty comes the strength to press on and the wisdom to make the right decisions to guard your future and freedom from the harsh consequences a sex crime conviction can bring. I consider it my job to begin the process of bringing certainty back into your life, so you can get back to normalcy and not have to constantly worry about what is coming around the corner related to your pending criminal matter.

In order to battle back against uncertainty, you must educate yourself on how the system works and what you can do to assist your attorney in the defense of your case. Once you know what your responsibility is and how your case will be defended, you and your attorney will work as a team to achieve the best possible result in your sex crime case.

DISCLAIMER

This publication is intended to be used for educational purposes only. No legal advice is being given, and no attorney-client relationship is intended to be created by reading this material. The author assumes no liability for any errors or omissions or for how this book or its contents are used or interpreted or for any consequences resulting directly or indirectly from the use of this book. For legal or any other advice, please consult an experienced attorney or the appropriate expert who is aware of the specific facts of your case and is knowledgeable of the law in your jurisdiction.

Hedding Law Firm

Los Angeles Criminal Defenders

(866) 986-2092

www.la-criminaldefense.com

TESTIMONIALS

"I hired Ron Hedding for my husband's criminal case. Ron made it simple for me and was honest from the gate as to what my husband was looking at. Ron was very helpful and answered any questions I had immediately by phone or email. In court they knew and respected Ron which gave me relief knowing that the right lawyer was on my husband's case. After everything, Ron was able to get years taken off my husband's time. Ron doesn't know how grateful we are to have met a humble lawyer and made it possible for my husband not have to miss a holiday or birthdays with his family. I would recommend Ron Hedding to everyone. He definitely gets the job done."

- Jasmin N.

****

"The Hedding Law Firm was amazing. They really took care of my needs and made sure they got the best results possible, in fact amazing results! I can't thank them enough. There are few times in life when you may need a lawyer, but when you do you want the Hedding team on your side. Thanks again."

- Joseph S.

****

"Honestly, I have never given a review to anybody, but HEDDING LAW FIRM. Definitely a yes!!! I give them a 1000%. They're amazing, plus efficient with a free consultation with Carlos. Within 30 minutes I had an answer. Thank you so much Carlos for taking my worries away. I will definitely be a returning client."

- Ceci R.

****

"I am so beyond happy with my experience with Ron. I had a lawyer prior to him that was so unsympathetic and horrible at communicating, so I decided to switch and I am so happy I did. Working with Ron was incredibly easy and communicating with him was never a problem. He's very personable and highly professional. The final outcome of my charges was beyond better than what I was expecting. I'm so entirely grateful for his work. I highly recommend him!"

- Britney P.

****

"Ron Hedding and staff have handled multiple cases for my employees. Over the past 20 years he has come through time and time again. He has always made time to speak directly with his clients and his support staff is just as attentive. His pricing is very reasonable for someone with his experience. I want to say thanks to you and the whole Hedding Law Firm staff!"

- Scott F.

****

"Googled criminal defense attorney and his name came up. I scheduled an appointment for a consultation. He gave me a forty-five-minute consult free of charge and gave me some very valuable advice. Tried to pay him for the hour but he refused. Love his set fee structure, with no hourly billing and no charging for every little thing!"

- Chris G.

****

Table of Contents

PERSONAL INTRODUCTION

Ronald D. Hedding is the founding member of the Hedding Law Firm. He has an extensive, well-rounded legal background in the area of criminal law. He has worked for the district attorney's office, a superior court judge, and as the guiding force behind the Hedding Law Firm. His multi-faceted experience sets him apart and puts him in an elite group of the best criminal defense attorneys in Southern California.

After establishing the Hedding Law Firm, Mr. Hedding dedicated himself towards the pursuit of zealously defending his clients to the highest professional standards. He has traveled all over this nation defending his clients and protecting their interests, reputations and freedoms. It is rare to find a criminal defense attorney with the dual ability to successfully fight a case in our jury system and the uncanny skills to negotiate a favorable disposition for his clients. It is even rarer to find an attorney with the wisdom to know the appropriate decision to make at the right time.

Mr. Hedding has been lead counsel in some of the most sensational criminal cases to be played out in Los Angeles County courthouses and at the federal level. He has received acclaim in newspapers, on the radio and in national publications. The key to Mr. Hedding's success- whether the case involves a DUI or murder charge- lies in his understanding of the US Criminal Justice System and the client's need to be informed of their best legal options so they can make the most informed decision in protecting their rights.

Current Employment Position(S)

- Managing Attorney

Bar Admissions

- U.S. Court of Appeals, 9th Circuit

- U.S. District Court Central District of California
- Superior Court for Los Angeles County
- U.S. Supreme Court

Honors and Awards

- Criminal Defense Attorney of the Year, The Editorial Staff of Consumer Business Review, 1999 - Present
- Accepted as Life Member of the National Registry of Who's Who, 2000 - Present
- Outstanding Professional Award for Dedicated Achievements in the Field of Criminal Law - ABI - USA, 2002 - Present
- Criminal Defense Attorney of the Year - The Editorial Staff of Consumer Business Review, 2003 - Present

Professional Associations and Memberships

- San Fernando Valley Bar Association, 1994 - Present
- America Bar Association, 1995 - Present
- Association of Trial Lawyers of America, 1998 - Present
- National Association of Criminal Defense Attorneys, 1999 - Present
- California Attorneys for Criminal Justice, 1995 - Present

Experience, Credentials, and Skills

- I have been named criminal defense attorney of the year in Los Angeles.
- I have won jury trials in all of the major courthouses in Los Angeles.
- My Los Angeles-based law firm is recognized by the Bar Register of Preeminent Lawyers as one of the top 5% of criminal defense law firms in Los Angeles County.
- I have been recognized in Los Angeles magazine as part of the Super Lawyers edition.
- I have won jury trials in Downtown Los Angeles federal courthouses.
- Top 5% of attorneys in California by Martendale Hubbel for ethics and legal ability.
- I have volunteered time working for the State Bar of California as a judicial nomination commissioner. I was responsible for investigating potential judges as part of a 38-person commission. I represented Los Angeles County in the process of selecting judges for the State of California.

- The president of the United States granted a presidential pardon for one of my Los Angeles-based clients.
- I have been involved in a published legal opinion related to a case that I have handled in one of the Los Angeles courts.
- As a Los Angeles defense attorney, I have written articles on criminal defense subject matters in local bar publications.
- AVVO has rated me Superb 10 out of 10 for skill and legal abilities in the Los Angeles courts.

CHAPTER 1
DEFINITION OF A SEX CRIME IN CALIFORNIA

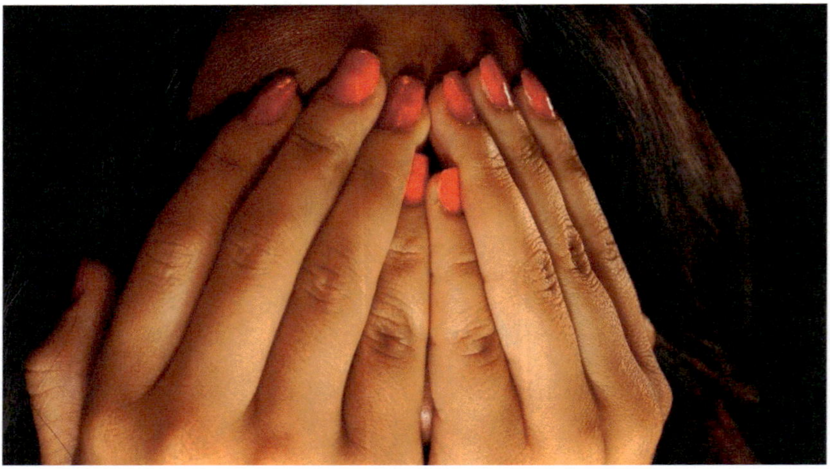

There is no perfect definition for sex crimes because there are so many different varieties of sex crimes that are listed in the penal code. However, in general, if someone is touching the intimate body part of another against that person's will, or if the person doesn't consent to it, then that would certainly be considered a sex crime. Also, you have to look at the category of minors in California, which are people under the age of 18. Those individuals cannot consent to any touching. Some people get confused and say, "The minor consented to it, they were okay with it." They cannot consent to it. Therefore, if someone were to touch the intimate body parts of a minor with the intent to sexually arouse that person, that would be a crime as well, and obviously that would be a very serious crime.

Sex Crimes That The Hedding Law Firm Handles

Over the course of the last 25 years, I have handled thousands of sex crime cases. I've pretty much defended people for just about every single sex crime related penal code violation. Some common ones that we see are sexual battery cases, which is penal code section 243.4. We also see a lot of P.C. 288 (a) charges, which deal with people who are involved with touching minors under the age of 18 in an inappropriate manner. I do a lot of federal child pornography cases in which people are doing things on the internet involving children and the FBI gets involved. I handle cases involving date rape. I handle cases in which people are being drugged for the purposes of sex, and the claim is that the defendant is the one who did it and then somehow violated that person sexually. So, I've handled countless types of cases, but it usually all boils down to whether or not the prosecutors can prove the particular sex charges, which boils down to whether or not they have the evidence.

People Involved In Sex Crimes

The majority of the sex crime cases that we see involve people who know each other, whether they are family members, people who are dating or people who are friends with one another. There are also cases that involve strangers touching people. I think the prosecutors and judges treat those types of cases much more harshly. Obviously, it's very serious when a stranger is violating somebody else's personal space in a sexual way. The prosecutors really come down hard on those offenders, and obviously I represent those individuals as well.

Do People Know They Are Being Investigated For A Sex Crime?

About half of the people are aware that they are being investigated for a sex crime. These people are called and the investigators want to talk to them, or the investigators show up at their house. The best scenario would be to not talk to them, even if the person is innocent. This is because things can be misinterpreted and misconstrued, people can be bullied or yelled at, and then the police can claim that they said something which will ultimately end up incriminating them. In the other half of the cases, the person doesn't know that they are being investigated. A lot of times what they'll do in these cases is something called a pre-text phone call, whereby the victim or the alleged victim will call the person and start asking them questions about the alleged sexual conduct, accusing them of the crime. The police will be on the other line listening and tape-recording, and then they will try to use that evidence later.

In either of these circumstances, if you have any suspicion that you might be investigated for any type of sex crime, then you want to get into a criminal defense attorney pre-filing. Make sure that your criminal defense attorney knows what's going on and can properly advise you on how to deal with the authorities. They can even contact the authorities on your behalf to let them know that you are represented, and that you are not going to be answering any questions unless your attorney is present.

CHAPTER 2
STEPS TO TAKE IF ARRESTED

The first thing you would want to do if you know you're being investigated or you've been arrested for a sex crime is speak to an attorney. Sit down, be honest with the attorney, go over the list of questions, and give them all of the information that you have. Your attorney is going to be your champion, and they know how to deal with these types of cases. One of the best investigative tools that the authorities have is getting the person to give them information and incriminate themselves. So, that's obviously not a good idea. Another thing that the authorities will do is have the alleged victim call the defendant, and they will record that call (which they're allowed to do). They will then feed the questions to the alleged victim so that the defendant incriminates themselves on tape.

The best first move is to get into contact with an attorney and be honest with them. Anything that you say under the privilege of the attorney-client relationship cannot be disclosed, whether or not you hire the attorney. You want to get in front of somebody who has done these types of cases before and has had success. Give them the path that you're about to go down so that they can really inform you of the best course of action.

What Are My Rights If I Have Been Arrested For A Sex Crime?

If you have been arrested for a sex crime, you have the right to remain silent. They are going to read your rights and tell you that you have a right to have an attorney present. Unfortunately, they don't have attorneys there at the jail, so that right is a bit of a fallacy. They don't want attorneys talking to you before they get a chance to talk to you. I've gone to jails when clients have hired me from the beginning, and I have been blocked from seeing my clients.

When I do get to see my client an hour later, my client tells me, "The detectives were here talking to me." They'll call the detectives, and then try to get a statement from the person before the attorney gets there. You have a right to not say anything, and that's usually the best thing to do in any type of situation where you're being charged with a sex crime. Ultimately, you are going to have a right to see everything against you, see who the witnesses are, see what the evidence is, and talk to an attorney about it before you enter any type of a plea or make any type of a move in the case.

Mistakes To Avoid In A Sex Crime Case

The biggest mistake to avoid is speaking to law enforcement. A lot of people think, "I didn't do anything wrong, they are not going to be able to prove anything against me, so why shouldn't I talk to them?" Unfortunately, I have seen too many times that the best evidence that the prosecutors end up having against a person in a sex crime case is their own statement. You're not going to be able to outsmart the police. They come in prepared because they're in the competitive business of ferreting out crime. They're going to be ready to ask you questions, respond when you deny things, and hit you with evidence that you don't think they have.

Again, if you're in a position where you can say something and if they don't tape-record it, then they can misconstrue what you say or later claim that you said certain things in a certain way when you did not. Then it's your word against the police officer's word, and it's your word against the alleged victim's word. In that scenario, you're not in a good situation. The best thing to do is say nothing.

CHAPTER 3
MISDEMEANOR OR FELONY?

The dividing line between misdemeanor and felony sex crimes is not as clear as we'd like it to be. The felony sex crime charges are typically going to be the more serious charges that involve children or violent sexual felonies, like rape or digital penetration. It may involve some other sex crime that is obviously against somebody's will and is a serious violation of that person's physical space. Misdemeanor sex crimes are usually going to be in the category of sexual batteries, like touching somebody in an intimate part of their body, assaults and other less serious misdemeanor type conduct, lewd conduct and solicitation. A crime in the misdemeanor category is not as violative of the person's body as a crime in the felony category.

A State Level Crime Or A Federal Level Crime?

There are a lot of sex crimes that could be charged at either the state or federal level. I think the difference is in regards to which types of cases the federal government chooses to take. The answer to that is that the federal government is usually dealing with child pornography cases or cases that are more sophisticated. I've seen large prostitution rings being dealt with by the federal government. The feds usually get involved in very sophisticated cases where they have to spend money and manpower in order to investigate and prosecute the case. The state is going to deal with simpler, more straightforward sex crimes, and the federal government is not going to waste their time or resources on those types of cases.

CHAPTER 4
ARE MOST SEX CRIMES BONDABLE OFFENSES?

Every sex crime is going to have some sort of bail attached to it, but it depends on what the crime is, how serious the crime is, the past criminal record, and what type of danger is posed to the society. If your sex crime case involves children and you pose a great danger to the society, then the judge can deviate from whatever the bail schedule is for that particular crime and set a higher bail if he or she believes that is appropriate.

The judges in Los Angeles have gone through all of the crimes that could be filed in LA County, and they've decided on what a reasonable bail is for those crimes. It is very rare that they would not set bail on a case at the state level. At the federal level, on the other hand, if you are charged with a crime and you're looking at a five, 10 or 15-year mandatory minimum, then the judges in those cases can just straight detain you. If that were the case, then you would not be able to get out and you would not be able to post a bond.

Penalties Associated With A Sex Crime In Los Angeles

You really can't generalize what the penalties are going to be for a sex crime. There are a variety of different sex crimes, and it depends on the type of crime that you plead to. It also depends on whether it's a felony or a misdemeanor, as well as your criminal record. The biggest thing that we're looking at when we defend these cases is whether or not they are going to make you plead to one of the listed crimes that require you to register as a sex offender for the rest of your life. We are also looking at whether they are going to try to make you go to prison or be on probation, and whether or not there is some other punishment besides custody time that we can get for you. We want to look at what type of restrictions they are going to put on you based on what you end up pleading guilty to. If you're innocent or not guilty of exactly what they're charging you with, then we have to decide whether or not we are going to take the case to trial.

How Often Does The Accuser Recant Allegations?

There are a lot of cases in which the accuser has second thoughts about prosecuting the defendant. But in a criminal case, it's not the accuser against the defendant, but rather it's the people or the state of California against the defendant. At the federal level, it's the federal government against the defendant. So, it's common for the accuser to have second thoughts, either because they embellished the story about the person or because they don't want to have to go through the embarrassment of testifying in a criminal case. Ultimately, the accuser not wanting the particular defendant prosecuted is only one of the factors related to the case. The prosecutors would be the ones who make the final decision on whether or not someone is going to be prosecuted and to what extent.

CHAPTER 5

CAN A CHARGE BE SUBSTITUTED FOR A SEX CRIME CHARGE?

There are many other charges that can be used in sex crime cases that do not require sex offender registration. However, the prosecutor and/or judge must be willing to allow the person to plea to one of those other charges that do not require sex offender registration. Whatever the person pleads to, it has to be something that makes sense in relation to what they are claimed to have done. In other words, they're not going to let somebody plead to a charge that has absolutely nothing to do with the behavior that led to their arrest in the first place.

This is where a seasoned sex crime attorney who's been doing this for a long time, has experience, and has dealt with the prosecutor and the judge in the courthouse where the case is pending comes in. That type of attorney will be able to craft these types of resolutions by coming up with a charge and convincing the prosecutor and judge to go with it.

Judges' And Prosecutors' Approach Towards Sex Crimes

Judges and prosecutors are harsh in prosecuting sex crimes because of politics, society, and the stigma that comes along with sex crimes. Unfortunately, there is a huge amount of stigma that comes along with sex crimes. A lot of society puts pressure on the legislature (which puts pressure on the courts) to make sure that people who are charged with sex crimes are treated harshly. That's why the prosecutors and judges are so harsh. Another reason is because these are the type of crimes that can come back and haunt prosecutors and judges if they are not harsh. If they are perceived to have given a particular defendant a break and that defendant commits another, more serious crime, then the authorities that get that case can question the judge or prosecutor. This can have serious political ramifications for the judge or prosecutor who gave the defendant a break.

What Determines If A Person Goes To Jail Or Not?

There are several factors that determine whether or not someone will go to jail for a sex crime. In general, those factors include the person's record for any prior sex crimes, the extent of their conduct, what they did, and how violative it was of the other person. The age of the alleged victim in the case is a huge factor in determining whether a person goes to jail or prison.

There is a difference between jail and prison. Jail refers to the county jail. It's considered local time, and it's usually very close to where the person committed the offense. Prison could be anywhere in the state of California if your crime occurs in LA County. Since the crimes are typically more serious for those offenders who get sentenced to prison, people generally serve more time in prisons than they do in jails. However, the setting is usually better because everyone knows what their sentence is and just wants to successfully complete it.

CHAPTER 6
SETTLEMENT OR TRIAL?

A lot of people ask me whether or not their case is going to go to trial. Ultimately, the decision as to whether or not a sex crime case goes to trial in Los Angeles will be made by the person who's been charged. If a case cannot be resolved with the prosecutors by way of negotiation, if your attorney can't convince the prosecutors to dismiss it, or if your attorney can't get it knocked out at the preliminary hearing level, then the judge and the prosecutor are going to say, "Okay, here is what you're offered to settle the case. If you don't want it, then you have to take the case to trial." The ultimate path is going to be to work out a deal, get the case dismissed, or take the case to trial.

If you don't want to work out a deal and the prosecutors will not dismiss the case, then the case will end up going to trial. The way that you decide if you want to take the case to trial is to talk to your attorney about it. Be honest with your attorney, give them all of the information, and let them assist you and educate you in making the best decision.

When To Take A Sex Crime Case To Trial?

It is feasible to take a sex crime case to trial when you have a good chance of winning. You don't want to take a sex crime case to trial if you don't have a good chance of winning it. This is because the consequences can be devastating. In determining whether or not you should take the case to trial, you want to sit down with a sex crime defense attorney who's been practicing for a long time, who has taken a lot of these cases to trial, and who understands how juries decide these types of cases. When you sit down with that attorney, you want to be honest with them and give them all of the information necessary to defend you. Pretend for a minute that you are the prosecutor or the police, and give them the information from that frame of reference. That way, they will be prepared to properly defend you and tell you what they feel might happen based on their prior experience of having defended these types of cases in front of juries.

How Is A Sex Crime Charge Going To Affect Me, My Family And Employment Prospects?

Unfortunately, when someone is charged with a sex crime, the authorities will get involved. If it's a sex crime that involves a minor and that person has minor children, then child services will often get involved and that person will be in jeopardy of losing their kids. If that happens, the children would be sent into the Monterey Park Children's Court, which is the child dependency court that handles matters in LA County.

Obviously, your job would only be affected if your employer found out about the charge or if your job somehow involved circumstances that would make it relevant for the employer to know that you're being charged with a particular sex crime. Under some circumstances, I do see the police alerting an employer who they feel needs to know in order to protect the public from a person's conduct. This is done on a case-by-case basis.

While the case is pending, you want to hire an attorney who can look out for these issues and be ready to defend you, not just in the court, but with the peripheral issues that can sometimes come along with a sex crime case in LA County.

Is A No-Contact Order Automatically Placed On The Accused In A Sex Crime Case In LA County?

I have seen over the past 25 years of handling sex crime cases that once the defendant appears in court, the judge will place a no-contact order on the defendant while the case is pending. That protective order is very broad, and typically encompasses contacting the person face-to-face, over the phone, at their job, or even having a third-party contact them on your behalf. If you do any of those things during the pendency of the case or during the pendency of the protective order that's in place, you will not only be subject to violating the terms of your bail or release, but also subject to being prosecuted for another crime. If you feel that the other party may do something to try to cause you to violate that protective order, then you should talk to your attorney. There is a strategy that can be employed to prevent this from happening.

CHAPTER 7
JURY SELECTION

In my experience, Los Angeles Courts have been fair when questioning potential jurors in a criminal case. When conducting the voir dire (which is where the judge and the lawyers ask questions to potential jurors), you really want to make sure you chose jurors who are going to be fair and keep an open mind. Everybody has their own history and their own baggage that they bring along. You don't want someone who has strong views on or a personal history with sex crimes, because that might cloud their judgment and prevent them from being fair. I am looking for people who are going to keep an open mind, listen to all of the evidence, and make the prosecutors prove their case. We want someone who will agree with me during the voir dire that if the prosecutors do not prove their case beyond a reasonable doubt, then they won't have a problem finding my client not guilty. Having a fair, open-minded jury gives the defense a fighting chance to win a case that has problems of proof.

CHAPTER 8
EVIDENCE AND WITNESSES

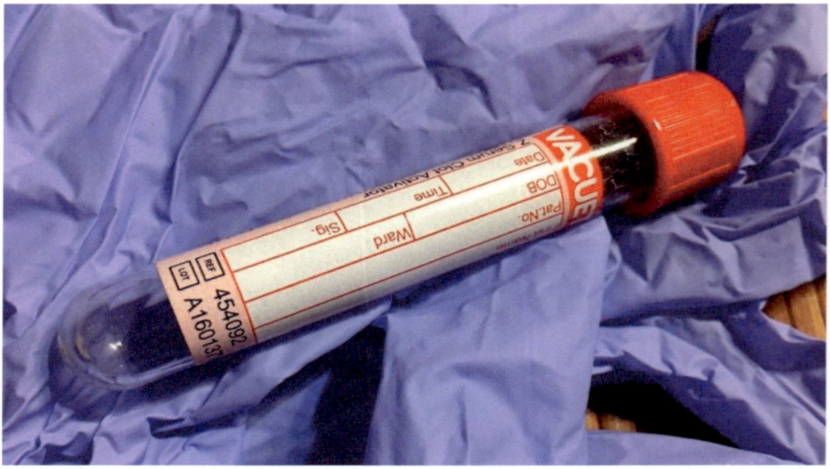

Most sex crime cases that I see do not involve experts or forensic evidence because it's basically a one-on-one situation; one person's claiming one thing, and the other is claiming another. There are a number of different factors that are utilized in order to attack the credibility of an alleged victim in that circumstance. However, there are cases that do involve DNA, experts, and forensic evidence. In these situations, we will need to get our own defense expert, especially if the prosecutors are relying on forensic evidence and experts. We will want to get someone who knows what they are doing, who has experience, and who can challenge the prosecutor's experts. If you go in there against the prosecutor's experts and you have no expert, then you are going to be in a very difficult position.

However, if you can get your own expert to refute the evidence of the prosecutor's expert (especially in DNA cases), then you are in a very strong position. I have DNA cases all the time, where my client is alleged to have done something to a victim in the case and it turns out that the DNA does not match up with what the alleged victim is claiming happened.

When you first look at the evidence, the DNA looks unbelievably strong, but then once our DNA expert looks at it, they say, "Wait a minute. First of all, this DNA is not very strong; it's a very weak sample. There are multiple DNAs found here, and there are a number of different reasons why this DNA could be here that are innocent." You definitely want to get an attorney who is familiar with this type of defense and who knows how to use experts to defend these types of cases.

Chapter 9
Defense Strategies

There are defenses to sex crimes. However, it's not a cookie-cutter situation where every defense applies in every case. The defenses that might be applicable will depend on the particular circumstances surrounding the crime. For example, sometimes people get involved with each other and both parties are drunk, or the alleged victim is drunk. The alleged victim wakes up the next morning and claims that the person did some inappropriate things, or they don't remember and they feel like they were taken advantage of. This could be a defense, because this doesn't necessarily mean that the other person took advantage of them. This type of situation spins on its own facts and it's something you need to discuss with your attorney.

Other times when I have seen sex crimes spun unfairly is when there is a divorce situation involved. For example, one spouse may accuse the other of some sort of sex-related incident in order to win money and gain a huge advantage over them in the divorce proceedings. Other areas where I see defenses that can be utilized are when the other party gets very jealous and angry, and then makes up a story against the person who ultimately gets arrested. There are a number of areas that can be utilized in order to establish a defense in a sex crime case. I've spoken to many police officers who realize that people make things up, and they don't tell the truth. The police are very savvy when it comes to this as well, and they are on the lookout for this type of stuff. They will listen to defense attorneys who have good arguments and the facts to support them.

Consent is another defense. If someone agrees to have sex with someone or permits someone to touch an intimate part of their body, then that would be a defense to a crime as long as it involved two adults. If there's a child involved, then the child cannot consent and that certainly could not be a defense in a sex crime case. Other defenses usually relate to the circumstances surrounding the sex offense, so they would be factually driven.

Sometimes people will try to take advantage of another person because there is a custody battle, so they claim some sort of a sex offense. Really what it boils down to is that there can be all sorts of defenses. It just depends on the charges and the circumstances. Obviously, the defense lawyer needs to speak to the client and find out their side of the story. Once this first step has been taken, a defense based on the facts given by the particular defendant can be established.

What Does The Defense Have To Prove In A Sex Crime Case?

Fortunately, in a sex crime case in Los Angeles, the defense doesn't have to prove anything. The prosecutor has the responsibility to not only prove sex crime cases, but also any criminal case in LA County. They have the burden to prove that the person is guilty of each of the elements and each of the charges beyond a reasonable doubt. The defendant has the presumption of innocence.

In other words, they are presumed innocent unless and until the prosecutors can prove them guilty.

A lot of times in sex crime cases, I will ask the jury if anyone thinks that my client is guilty just because they walked in here and can see that they are being charged with a sex crime. Believe it or not, a lot of people raise their hands. Before the trial starts, this becomes the opportunity to explain to the jury that the person is presumed innocent.

I tell the jury that if they had to vote right now, then they would have to vote not guilty because of that presumption of innocence. In a clear, strategic and lawful way, I also ask them how they would like it if they were charged with a crime that they didn't commit, and the jury came in already thinking that they were guilty. That's not how our American system works; that's not right, and there is a presumption of innocence. The prosecutors must prove their case beyond a reasonable doubt, or you should be found not guilty.

CHAPTER 10
SEX CRIMES INVOLVING DRUGS AND ALCOHOL

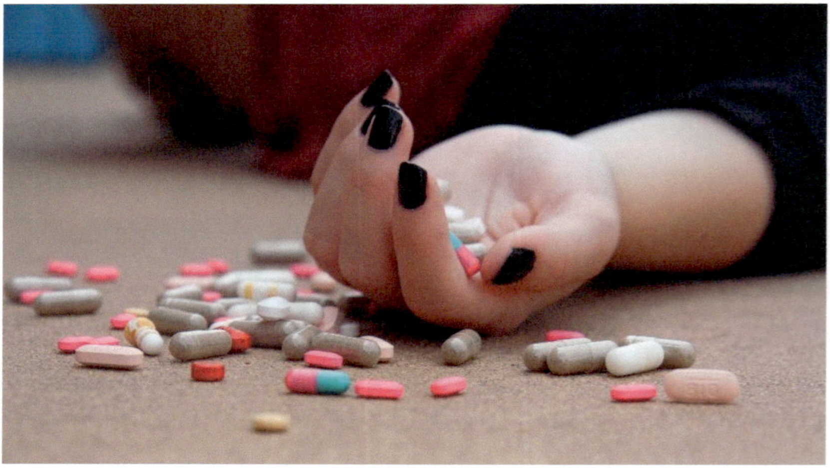

Prosecutors, defense attorneys and judges handle sex crime cases in Los Angeles that involve drugs and alcohol differently. The reason is because when people do not have full command of their faculties due to the consumption of drugs or alcohol, then that will affect both their memory and the prosecutor's ability to convict someone. If, on the other hand, a person is claiming that they were given some sort of drug that they didn't know about, then that's a different type of case that is handled by special prosecutors in Downtown LA. You're going to want to get a very sophisticated defense lawyer to defend you in that circumstance.

Cases that involve drugs and alcohol happen all the time. They are probably the majority of sex crime cases that are filed. You need to get an attorney who is experienced, who's dealt with these cases in LA County, who knows how to defend them, who knows how to point out the problems when people use drugs and alcohol, and who then tries to piece together what happened. Instead of piecing together with good solid detailed information, the police are speculating and trying to get someone in trouble for a crime that oftentimes they didn't commit.

CHAPTER 11
REGISTRATION AS A SEX OFFENDER

Not every sex crime conviction is going to require the offender to register as a sex crime offender. There is a list of sex crimes in Los Angeles that, if plead guilty to, require you to register as a sex offender for the rest of your life. There is also a list of sex crimes for which there is a requirement for limited registration. As we make this information available today, there is a proposal that looks like it's going to pass. There's going to be a three-tiered system related to registration for sex crimes in California. Once that system is implemented, it'll be much clearer who has to register and the extent of the registration. It will be easier to know whether a person's going to be on the Megan's Law website or restricted from going to different areas. If you're going to have to plead guilty to a sex crime, it's crucial that you know whether or not you'll have to register as a sex offender, what the extent of the registration is going to be and what the ramifications are going to be.

If someone has to plead guilty to a sex charge, we try to find a sex crime that is non-registerable. There are actually not that many, but there is a list of them. If we can show the prosecutor that it's more appropriate for you to plead to a non-registerable offense, then obviously we are going to save you a lot of aggravation and that horrible negative stigma of having to register as a sex offender.

Restrictions That A Registered Sex Offender Faces In California

There are a number of different restrictions when it comes to having to register as a sex offender. These restrictions depend on what type of crime you committed and what category you find yourself in relation to sex registration. The key we should be striving for is clarity and knowing exactly what you can and can't do, so that you do not find yourself on the wrong side of the law.

We don't want you lumped with everybody else who has to register for life. The more serious the sex crime, the more restrictions there will be. The type of restrictions for the most serious offenders include having their picture and information on the internet, and being restricted to staying out of public locations such as parks and other areas where a lot of people or minors tend to be. It depends on the circumstances of the conviction, what type of a resolution was negotiated, and what the judge sentenced them to. It's going to depend on how new legislation takes effect—hopefully the new legislation will make it very clear and define exactly what people who have to register as sex offenders in Los Angeles County can and can't do.

Getting Off The Sex Offender Registry

There are a number of different things that can be done to get off the sex offender registry, depending on when the person was convicted of the sex crime and what the sex crime was. What you are looking to do is obtain a certificate of rehabilitation or a governor's pardon. I have negotiated and seen cases where the person has to register as a sex offender just for the probationary period. Under these circumstances, they would be able to get out of the registration requirement if they can get a certificate of rehabilitation. You can talk to an attorney who is experienced with sex crimes and sex crime legislation, or to the people who are in charge of the sex crime registration.

Can A Sex Offense Conviction Be Expunged In Los Angeles County?

There are sex offenses that can be expunged. As far as sealing records, that's a juvenile term. You can seal and destroy juvenile records, but adult cases in California must be expunged / dismissed. Unfortunately, there is no such thing as a true expungement in California. If you are able to get any crime in California expunged, it would still show on your record when somebody ran you with the Department of Justice, though it would show as dismissed. The courts have started to call expungements "dismissals" instead of expungements, so that nobody gets confused about it.

That's a completely separate issue that has to be dealt with on the level of getting a certificate of rehabilitation, some sort of a governor's pardon, or your attorney going to court and getting the judge to terminate your probation if you only have to register during the probationary period.

CHAPTER 12
HIRING AN EXPERIENCED ATTORNEY

Sex crime cases are some of the most serious cases there are. You want someone who does them frequently, because each of the courts has their own special unit that just handles sex crimes. They are called sex crime prosecutors. If a person is not familiar with defending sex crimes in LA County, they are going to be at a huge disadvantage in dealing with the sex crime prosecutors. They are already at a disadvantage because there are different rules for bail and sentencing. There are a lot of different components and a lot of different moving parts when it comes to a sex crime case, and you need to have an attorney who has been down the path you are about to travel and had success. You need an attorney who knows how to deal with the personalities that you have to deal with, including the prosecutors, judges, and law enforcement personnel. Law enforcement agencies have special sex crime units as well, and they are in the competitive business of arresting those individuals they suspect of committing sex crimes.

You definitely want to have someone who has handled sex crime cases. I have been handling sex crime cases for the past 25 years. I worked for a superior court judge, and I have seen how they deal with these types of cases. I have also worked for the district attorney's office, and I see how they deal with sex crime cases. I have had my own criminal defense practice since the early 1990s dealing with sex crimes, seeing how to win them, what it takes to negotiate them, and how to get the best possible resolution for my clients while taking into consideration their family, their job, their reputation and their freedom!

The Right Time To Hire An Attorney

If you think you're going to be charged with a sex crime, you should absolutely hire an attorney as soon as humanly possible. The bottom-line is this: the authorities aren't going to arrest you and prosecute you based on the fact that you hired an attorney. Hiring an attorney does not suggest that you are guilty. The authorities are going to arrest you if they think they can prove the case against you. Whether you hire an attorney or not, the dividing line between the charges being filed and not being filed has to do with the evidence. So, by hiring an attorney, you can make sure that you don't give them any evidence that might incriminate you. Sometimes the attorney can actually provide them with evidence that shows that you're innocent of the crime, or else mitigate the crime down to something much less serious than what you would normally be charged with.

Can Someone Ever Represent Themselves In A Sex Crime Case?

Someone can represent himself or herself in a sex crime case, but it's absolutely ridiculous and it's extremely dangerous to try this. Sex crimes are such serious crimes and carry with them such large sentences (including life in prison) that to represent yourself is extremely dangerous. If you go to trial, represent yourself and lose, the judge is going to perceive you not only as someone who committed a sex crime, but as someone who really doesn't care about the system, doesn't think to get an attorney to represent them, and basically just beats to their own drum. That's probably the most dangerous person from the court's perspective, as far as sex crimes go. And, the sentence the court doles out will be harsh for these offenders.

In addition, it's foolish to represent yourself because you are not a lawyer, you don't know what motions can be brought to defend yourself, and you don't know when you should negotiate a case and when you should try a case. If you do decide to try the case, you don't know how to cross-examine witnesses like seasoned sex crime attorneys do, you don't know when to try and block the prosecutor's evidence, what evidence is appropriate and what evidence is not, and you are probably not going to know how to put evidence on the right way in your own defense.

Social Stigma Associated With Sex Crime Cases In California

People should realize that when you are charged with a sex crime case, there is such a stigma in society today that the pendulum has swung very far against people who are charged with sex crimes. People can be completely innocent of the crime, or the prosecutors can overcharge the crime. People that I have talked to and that I have defended feel alone until they get an attorney on their side. They feel like everybody is against them, and everybody assumes they are guilty before they even hear any of the evidence. It's crucial to get someone who is battle-tested, who has been down the road that you are about to travel, who knows how to handle these cases, and who has the wisdom, experience, and the skill to make the right decision for you, and to guide you in the best possible direction.

What's The Next Step?

You should be getting a list of questions to ask your prospective attorney in preparation for a face to face meeting. I meet with all of my clients myself, and I litigate every aspect of sex crime cases because of the serious nature of these charges. The goal that I have in the meeting is to understand what happened in regards to my client's arrest and come up with a game plan moving forward so the client knows what they can do to help me defend them. That way, we both know exactly what our target outcome is for the successful resolution of the case.

The one key thing that I ask my clients for from the beginning is that they are completely truthful with me about what happened, so we do not have any surprises during the pendency of the case and so I can most effectively represent them. I believe it is my job to be more prepared than the prosecutor and the judge so that I can utilize every possible advantage at the client's disposal. We will only have one chance to do it right and make sure you never have to deal with this situation again.

Once you meet with me face to face, you will have a solid feel for what the parameters of your case are and what you can expect to achieve. I will be straight forward and honest with you so that you truly have a feel for where you stand and what you can realistically hope to achieve. It is crucial that we have a meeting of the minds from the beginning of the representation so we both feel comfortable with where we are heading in the defense of your case.

INDEX

S

V

NOTES

Made in the USA
Monee, IL
05 November 2026

67383932R00038